A Bad Smell

Written by Jack Gabolinscy
Illustrated by Daron Parton

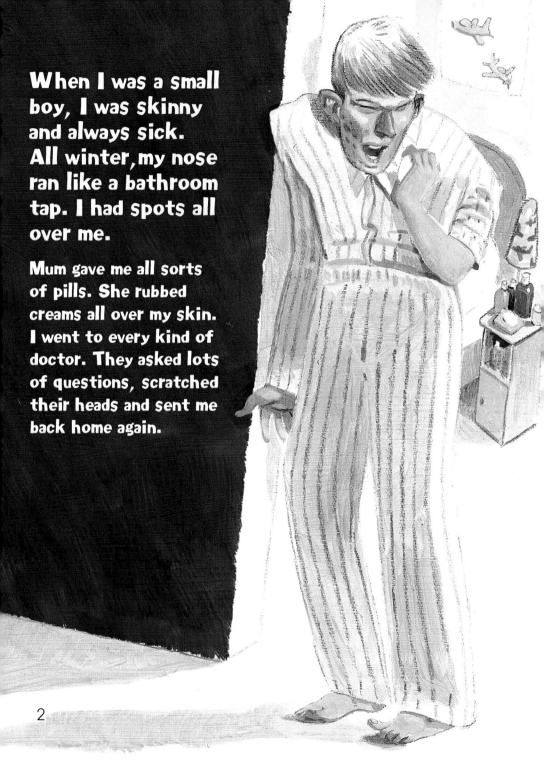

When I was a small boy, I was skinny and always sick. All winter, my nose ran like a bathroom tap. I had spots all over me.

Mum gave me all sorts of pills. She rubbed creams all over my skin. I went to every kind of doctor. They asked lots of questions, scratched their heads and sent me back home again.

We didn't have much money, but Mum made food fit for a king. She grew vegetables of every kind. She baked bread and cakes and made ice cream. And we always had fresh fruit.

But it was all a waste of time. I ate like a bird. I picked at my meals until they got cold on my plate. I looked like a skeleton with my skinny arms and legs.

My big brother and I were really different. He was strong and had big muscles. I was a skinny little runt. The kids at school called us . . .

Muscle and Bones

"Hey, Bones!" my brother would say to me, laughing. "When are you going to put some muscle into that skin?"

I got tired of being sick. Ten minutes stuck in bed was like being in jail. But, when I got hives, I did like having cream all over my face and arms. I looked like a spotted space alien.

"What is it this time, Jack?" the teacher asked once.

"Don't know, Miss. Something called contagious I think."

The teacher ran out of the room like a Mars-bound rocket. She came back a few minutes later. "No, Jack," she said. "We called your mother. It's not contagious. It's just hives from eating a tomato when you're not supposed to."

One day, when he was poking my tummy and tapping my bones, the doctor said, "You could go to a health camp. It would be good for you. It would put some fat on your bones."

So I went to a health camp by the sea. I shared a bunkhouse with other boys. They all liked me because I could pull my tummy in so far that my ribs stuck out.

7

On the first day of camp, our group went fishing. We dug in the sand for shellfish to use for bait. Then we put our lines into the water. I was the only one who caught a fish. It was a small fish, but I thought it was huge.

I took it back to camp and gave it to the cook in the kitchen. "Can you cook it for me, please?" I asked.

"I can't cook this fish," said the cook. "It's too small. Look! It's even skinnier than you are."

Just then, the bell rang for lunch. I quickly put the fish away in the bunkhouse and went to the lunchroom to eat.

9

On the third morning of my stay, the camp leaders did a bunkhouse check. We waited while they checked that everything was OK.

"Good," said one of the leaders. Then she turned to the other leader. "Can you smell something?" she asked.

"No," replied the other leader. "I can't smell anything."

The next morning, the same thing happened. On the fifth morning, the first leader came into the bunkhouse and sniffed loudly.

"Poof!" she said. "There is a bad smell in this bunkhouse. It stinks. It's awful."

The two camp leaders sniffed up and down the bunkhouse. They stopped by my bed.

"It's near here," said one.

The other followed her nose like a sniffer dog hunting a rabbit. She came to my locker. "It's in here," she said.

The two leaders took the clothes from my locker and put them on my bed. One of them got on her hands and knees and took my shoes and boots from the bottom shelf. When she stood up again, she was holding my dead fish. "Whose locker is this?" she asked.

"Mine," I said. Everyone looked at me. I wrapped my arms around my skinny chest.

I waited for the end to come. The leaders looked at each other. They looked cross. What were they going to do?

Then the leaders started to laugh. They held their sides and laughed until tears ran down their faces. Soon we were all laughing.

Then one of the leaders picked up my clothes. "Come with me, Jack," she said. "We need to wash all your clothes now."

We put my clothes in the washing machine, and then she took me to the kitchen. "You look as if you need a good feed," she said. I had a feast of buns, cake and a chocolate milkshake.

"You won't leave another fish in your locker, will you?" she asked, laughing again.

"No way," I replied.

I enjoyed my stay at the health camp. When I went back home, I was pleased with myself. I hadn't coughed or scratched or felt sick once. And I had a camp certificate. I was a winner.

Health Camp Certificate

This is to declare that

Jack Gabolinscy

is a winner.

He put on 5 kilograms in weight during his stay at Health Camp.

Signed _Medical Smithee_

"Wow!" said Mum. "You've put on weight. And you haven't felt sick once?"

"Well, Mum," I replied. "I've got a sore stomach right now."

"What? Where does it hurt?" asked Mum.

"My pants are too tight. I'm too fat for my pants!"

17

- **where** the story is set.

Who	When	Where
	When I was a small boy.	

A recount tells what happens.

A recount has a **conclusion**.

Guide Notes

Title: A Bad Smell
Stage: Fluency

Text Form: Recount
Approach: Guided Reading
Processes: Thinking Critically, Exploring Language, Processing Information
Written and Visual Focus: Speech Text, Text Highlights

THINKING CRITICALLY
(sample questions)
- What do you think this story could be about? Look at the title and discuss.
- Look at the cover. What do you think the bad smell might be?
- Look at pages 2 and 3. How do you think the doctors felt when they couldn't figure out what was wrong with Jack? Why do you think this?
- Look at pages 4 and 5. What do you think *food fit for a king* means?
- Look at pages 6 and 7. Why do you think Jack liked looking like a *spotted space alien*?
- Look at pages 8 and 9. Why do you think Jack thought the fish he caught was huge?
- Look at pages 10 and 11. What other things do you think the camp leaders would be checking for?
- Look at pages 12 and 13. How was Jack feeling? How do you know this?
- Look at pages 14 and 15. What sort of people do you think the camp leaders were? Why do you think this?
- Look at pages 16 and 17. How do you know Jack was pleased with himself?

EXPLORING LANGUAGE

Terminology
Spread, author and illustrator credits, imprint information, ISBN number

Vocabulary
Clarify: health camp, certificate, locker, bunkhouse, hives, contagious
Adjectives: *skinny* arms, *spotted* space alien, *bad* smell
Pronouns: I, she, we, me, she, they, you
Adverbs: *quickly* put the fish away; sniffed *loudly*
Similes: I ate *like a bird*, I looked *like a spotted space alien*
Focus the students' attention on **homonyms**, **antonyms** and **synonyms** if appropriate.